How to Convert Online

-

The #1 Guide to Split-Testing, Email Marketing, Sales Pages and Lead magnets

-

by

Lisa Sutherlan

Table of Contents:

An Introduction:

Most businesses approach conversion as the last piece of the puzzle inside of business. They work hard in setting up a website, developing an audience, and generating traffic to get their website up and running.

After it looks like everything is smooth sailing, business owners begin to realize that there's a lot more to making money online than being popular.

Understanding how to sell products and services will determine whether any business thrives or fails. While there have been rapid advancements in the understanding of what convinces s a potential customer to buy a product, 2017 is a year where marketers understand the power and value of classic sales strategies.

This guide to conversion is all about understanding the unconscious emotional drivers of your customers and learning how to capitalize on human behavioral patterns.

The strategies presented in this book are simple and applicable. They are considered extremely effective strategies for generating sales and building a successful business.

Online business has the power to transform lives, but only if that business converts prospective buyers into happy clients. By being capable of selling, a whole new door opens up for business owners.

Here are 7 Powerful Benefits Of Business Conversion:

Focusing on Conversion Grants Inside Access to Customers.

By shifting our attention to conversion, we're automatically forced to step outside of personal biases that can naturally come with owning a business.

Through paying special attention to your prospective customers, we can begin to tap into the underlying emotions and problems of any industry.

By nature, humans have negative experiences that occur throughout every stage of their life. By identifying what the market is responding to, any business can gain insights into how to market, promote and present products and information to customers. Every market is unique and dynamic creating hundreds of "untapped" opportunities for every audience inside of every industry.

Strategy for Gaining Inside Access to Customers:

If you've read the first two books in the 2017 series, you've already gained incredible insight into the foundations of researching customers. If you haven't read the first two books, here's a nice strategy that will allow you discover more about your customer.

Step 1: The Discovery Process

Practically every industry has a community. This includes blogs, social groups, magazines, and forums.

By investigating these outlets, any online business can discover what inspires their prospective customers. Whether you're looking to address big issues or are simply trying to make life more enjoyable, reading through online hubs will give any business insights to successful approaches in marketing.

Tailoring products and services to what the community is trying to accomplish is a powerful first step in making a sale. Here's a simple process to discovering the major talking points of any market.

-Do a quick search for popular blogs inside your industry and create an RSS feed system to pay attention to what content gets shared and where the discussion creates engagement.

Cruise through the RSS feed and look at what content gets exposure. Every time you find a piece of media that creates responses and engagement, save it into a specialized folder. This folder will give you inside access to tools and strategies that you can use inside of your sales process.

-Hit the forums and look for some active threads. Look at what people are looking for and what questions they are asking. Copy and paste the most active threads, reactions and questions into a document and save the collection into a folder.

While there's no substitution for surveying your customers, most online business owners don't have access to a huge database of customers to survey. Understanding what directions conversations develop in forums allows any business to discover emotional triggers that spark reactions.

-Look into Facebook Groups and Twitter Communities. Raw and powerful stories wreck havoc on social servers like wildfire. When a community gets wild up about a certain topic, it's best for you and your business to take notice and try to capitalize on traffic as quickly as possible.

By keeping up with what's buzzing inside of your industry you'll be able to discover subtle sales pitches and benefits that you may have previously overlooked. The social landscape is a wonderful way to generate tons of content that you can use to get featured on popular websites, marketing to your own website, become a conversation starter inside multiple online communities, and even generate more direct traffic to your website.

This is a very basic strategy, but the effects are incredible when it comes to conversion. The fact of the matter is that no one will buy a product unless he or she feels a connection to it. Discovering what your industry cares about it the first step in creating conversion through online business.

1. **Conversion Brings Customers to Life.**

When you create an online business, it can get hard to connect with your audience on a personal level. That's why it's so crucial to bringing your customer to life. Jay Abraham introduced the marketing world to a concept called Preeminence.

Preeminence is a strategy that should be used as the fundamental principle inside of your sales efforts. It declares that when someone hits the busy button, you become their most trusted adviser.

If you're looking to develop a business that converts enough to make sustainable profits, your attitude needs to grasp a shift in perspective towards a ground-breaking business model. The truth is that a lot of people are looking for leadership inside of their lives. They are searching for someone to go to so that they can fix their problems or fulfill their desires.

It's important when you build a business to take your customers seriously and to treat them as dear friends and clients. Your goal in business should be the medium of change for your clients.

Transform yourself and your business so that you and your website becomes prominent and cherished by your clients. Humans don't like to look at life as a giant process to get to where they want to be.

They like to understand where they are currently and want the feelings of a solution to fulfill their negative emotions. When you set out to achieve preeminence, your only goals should be to transform someone's emotional state. To make them feel special through providing solutions that are uniquely tailored to their situation.

People don't like taking action, so it's important to sell your strategies just as hard as you do the results inside of your business. When you convince a viewer to take action, you have become your client's trusted adviser; when a customer takes enough action to produce results, you'll have transformed someone's life.

Once you sell the power of action to improve your client's life, you have the power to bring them to life and to make some income as an exchange.

How to Bring Clients to Life.

1. When you're trying to bring your customer to life, remember to use the perspective of preeminence as your framework. Imagine that you're every prospective client's most trusted adviser. Genuinely care what's best for them and understand how your clients tick.

2. Create a customer avatar.

Creating a customer avatar is the perfect way to bring thousands of statistics to life. When you begin to understand that your audience is a series of people with similar thinking and emotional structures, you'll be able to identify similar characteristics to create what experts call a customer avatar.

A customer avatar is an individual that is created by a business to capture an exact demographic. This individual is a fictional character that holds the characteristics of your market. By giving these people a face, you transform your market from a crowd into a person you can talk to and communicate with at an individual level.

How to make a customer avatar.

Developing a customer avatar is an in-depth process. The elements involved include:

1. Values
2. Culture
3. Social Engagement

4. Experiences in life

5. Age

6. Gender

7. Marital Status

8. Hair color, eye color, height, weight, facial structure and body type.

9. The type of technology they enjoy

Combine these characteristics into a detailed bio for your avatar's life.

Developing multiple avatars. A weighted system.

One sales pitch won't work for everyone. This is where building multiple avatars come into play. By having a set of 4 or 5 customer avatars, you'll be able to capture more of the market and create powerful responses inside of your sales pitches. Over time, these avatars can shift and transform to create new additions to the team. While you test out which avatars are most effective you can distribute more weight to the successful avatars.

How to use your customer avatars.

Before you create content, products, and sales pages, imagine running idea you have through your avatars and ask them how you can improve on your ideas and whether or not they'd enjoy engaging with your content. This will give you a perfect place to move to after you engage in the discovery process.

3. Conversion allows owners to treat business opportunities seriously.

Once you invest in creating a profitable sales pitch, the game changes forever. It means that every dollar you can invest makes money and that every time you succeed in giving your business exposure, you make more money. Once you have successfully developed a sales funnel that's successful, your business transforms into a living machine that cashes in the money like auto-pilot. When you can convert prospects into clients, the business world changes. Traffic doesn't become another tool, it becomes a way to make money off of doing things you love. And isn't that what this business is all about?

Unlike the employment world, business is all about $/hour. In order to make enough money to pay the bills, buy a new home and take a couple of wonderful trips around the world, money must be made. The days of working hard to create a paycheck are gone. Instead, it's important to work smarter while you keep up the hard work.

This is where conversion comes into play. While it does take time and attention to detail, spending 100 hours on a couple of sales pages will benefit any business owner for years. That would translate to 10 hours a week across 10 weeks. That seems like a massive investment of time without making a single $. However, shifting your attention to marketing a successful product for 100 weeks becomes a game changer. Imagine that from that point forward, all a business owner had to do to become successful is push 5,000 visitors to a product that costs $49 and has a conversion rate at 5%. The income generated from that product would be $12,250/month. This situation becomes even more promising when the sales are generated on auto-pilot.

When the only job of business owners is to promote a profitable product or service, a switch flips for them. Online business shifts from being a "law of attraction" fairy tale into a practical and enjoyable job. Everything becomes serious. In the example above, every visitor is worth $2.45. And every wave of 100-1,000 prospects that are captured creates healthy weekly profits for small online business owners.

By taking conversion seriously and making it a number one priority, anyone can make money online. If you've put in all of the hard work, this is the last step in the puzzle before you market more.

4. Conversion Transforms Novices into Pros.

Something powerful happens when professionals use conversion statistics to run their businesses. When an owner has an understanding of what the market wants, he or she will be able to develop a safety net around new marketing strategies. New ads can be costly and dangerous to young businesses. However, having an understanding of what sparks engagement inside of an industry gives businesses inside access to what phrases and hooks would be successful. After the discovery process, the only thing stopping businesses from succeeding is trial and error.

Bringing prospects to life and following statistics allows businesses owners to shift their mindset from being a guru into being an unbiased and trusted adviser. Conversion takes the emotional roller coaster out of whether or not a product or service will work and how to improve products and services in the future. Sometimes a single word can change everything when it comes to conversion. Maybe the idea was phenomenal but the impact wasn't delivered. Maybe people are looking for a different emotional trigger when it comes to investing in a product.

The truth is not every product is going to be perfect on its first go around, but by focusing on conversion any business owner can take statistical feedback to observe whether or not an ad or sales pitch is working.

5. **Conversion Gives Businesses Confidence.**

Becoming obsessed with conversion optimization is one of the greatest triumphs a business owner can undertake. Having a valid business product makes rookies look prominent and season vets look unstoppable. When you develop conversion mindset, you'll think differently, develop a different posture and even speak more confidently. When you talk to other business owners or set down to write a new marketing piece, you'll be confident that you'll succeed. In online business, most businesses never truly launch off the ground. The number one identified reason for this pure habitual habit. When people choose to take on any endeavor, they feel motivated and confident that they'll transform their lives. However, after a couple of weeks, most people loose steam and begin to hesitate. Doubts begin to arise that a market is already tapped out or the products they have to offer aren't actually wanted. Focusing on conversion and bringing great products to the table is the best way to restore confidence and eliminate doubt from the business.

6. Conversion Brings Networking to Life.

When a business has a product that takes cash out of wallets, almost every marketer will want in on the action. That means automatic money for you. In previous books, we talked about the importance of networking and understanding your market. But when the time comes to get featured on other websites, it may have been a bit nerve-wracking. Your approach will certainly shift when you have successfully developed a product that makes money. You'll feel more justified being put into the spotlight and you'll produce some incredible content that will allow traffic to flood from other businesses into yours.

What's better is that if you put your product on affiliate websites, you'll be able to make money without even conversing with some marketers. By using conversion as a main marketing tool inside of networking, content creation, and sales, you'll quickly find yourself as an authority inside of the market. That's a great situation to be in if you approach your business through the strategy of preeminence listed in the Bringing Your Customers to Life section above.

7. Conversion Research Creates More Back End Sales.

There's no better feeling than the first time a prospect becomes a client. However, all too often, these clients become one time buyers after they leave your website. Through the study and research that's necessary to develop successful products, services, and sales pitches, you'll undoubtedly think of ground-breaking products you can offer your current clients to make even more improvements inside of their lives.

You'll be able to test introductory products, premium courses, and even live workshops to boost your back end sales.

If you're hesitant on what makes a winning product, you can use the guide below to help you boost front-end conversion as well as make a killing months and even years after you acquire a client.

Product Splintering

Product splintering is the easiest way to transform one product into an opt-in, a trip-line, and a premium product. This strategy was introduced from Digitalmarketer and is a proven and methodical sales strategy that allows businesses to create a sales funnel that increases front end and back end sales. The most important money in creating clients is convincing them to open their wallet. Acquiring a penny from 100 customers is drastically more powerful than acquiring $49 from a single customer. Believe it or not, the first step in selling a more expensive product is through convincing a potential client to become a customer in the first place.

Through a combination of opt-ins, a combination of low priced pitches, and main product hooks, you'll be able to build a product line that creates better results than you thought possible. Here's how Digitalmarketer breaks down their sales pitches.

1. Lead Magnets: Lead magnets are the roots of conversion. Lead magnets are quick but powerful solutions that will transform the prospects life within 10 a minute read or less. These are basically the magic bullet that people are looking for. Examples include "how I lost 20 pounds while eating pizza", "how to get your first 1,000 subscribers free", "loose a pound a day through this revolutionary hack", etc. The key to lead magnets is to create a fantastic teaser for the program you're about to pitch.

2. Every flagship product is made up of key components. For example, an online business course will be built with 3. These components include website

production, product development, and marketing. Every one of these 3 key components has 7 major strategies that create a system that brings the key components to life. In other words, when you have a complete product, you can choose from 21 different options as the foundations of a trip wire.

A trip wire is a small priced product that will feature the type of content that makes up your flagship course. For example, a trip wire for an online business course would be one of seven key strategies for generating products and services that convert.

3. The third product inside of the product splintering is your flagship product. It's the identity of your information and a direct solution to the major problems that your clients face inside of their lives. These solutions are geared as overall products that generate major transformations.

In other words, these products sell major shifts in experiences like replacing income, finding a perfect mate, creating happiness. The major job of these products is to transform the "flaws" of clients into strengths. The lead magnet and the trip wire are considered surface solutions. They produce pleasant sensations quickly and efficiently. However, main products, or flagship products, are considered as stable, long-term solutions that will transform challenges into positive habits for your clients.

For more information on product development, you can use these sources as a guide:

- Make sure you watch all 3 marketing videos in the link below if you'd like the full effect.

https://www.youtube.com/watch?v=k51vFkjtf3g

-Here's more about product splintering!

http://www.digitalmarketer.com/customer-value-optimization/

-Here's a quick guide to making products fast! https://gkic.com/blog/information-marketing/6-steps-to-creating-info-products-super-quickly/

Chapter 1: The Power Of Email Marketing

What Makes Email Marketing so Powerful?

Why is email marketing so important and why should you use it?

When it comes to online business, having access to a large and responsive list is the equivalent of owning the world's largest gold mine. Here are 10 major factors that make email the lord of online conversion.

Benefit 1: Grants the ability to send mail directly into the pockets of clients.

When you acquire an email, you instantly gain access to a prospect in a place they are most likely to be responsive. If you have an email on your phone, you'll already realize that you can access your emails anywhere. You can read emails during downtime at home, work, during breaks, on walks, hang out with friends and even at the DMV.

In 2017 a large portion of prospective buyers uses emails kind of like a customized magazine. Every day, they can receive access to specialized solutions that can fix any aspect of life without taking the time to research. Over time, people develop an attachment to this newsfeed the same way they would a social media profile. Due to this simple observation, capturing an email should be every business owner's number one priority. An email gives an online business man the chance to entertain, impact and transform clients lives. It's a series of awesome reminders about how great life actually is and how to make it even better. To some people, the right email subscriptions can create the perfect substitution for reading books and watching television.

Through email, a smartphone user can create a fully immersive experience delivered directly to their pocket. This includes videos, conversations, entertainment and emails.

This new era delivers an operating system that's more profitable to marketers than tech lovers could have ever imagined.

Benefit 2: Gives the chance to test hundreds of sales tactics to thousands of clients.

What's better than being able to send 100 specialized messages to thousands of prospective customers. Well, that's exactly what you get when you gain access to a great email marketing list. No matter how much research and leg work you put in up front, the truth of the matter is that it's almost impossible to create the highest converting pitches after the first couple of reps. Luckily, owning an email list allows a business owner to take hundreds of angles and combination of marketing tactics. It's basically a giant web of connecting words, pain points, ideas and experiences that are infinitely interchangeable. When a business owner gains access to a list, they essentially unlock thousands of hours of research to be tested and measured by automatically by a machine.

Benefit 3: Allows the opportunity to connect with customers at a personal level.

When people are reading content that's broadcasted for the world to see, they experience an entirely different state than when they receive emails tailored to a series of "one-on-one" conversations. When you have the chance to email someone, you get the chance to bring your products and your business to life. Email is a sanctuary for both marketers and clients inside of every industry. It allows clients and advisers to connect over a period of time rather than a single moment. In turn, flashy bullet points have the chance to become dynamic stories, and products can be brought to life. When the experience of stories becomes a prominent factor, a shift in thinking occurs inside of the minds of clients. Products change from a strategy to extract money to an opportunity to access more stories and to create positive and transformational experiences.

Benefit 4: Generates money automatically.

Even though this is a flashy benefit to email marketing, it's impossible to ignore how incredible it is to be able to write one series of emails and then automatically replicate it thousands of times to extremely targeted clients. As your business gains traction, you'll start realizing that you're making money from places that you weren't expecting. You may have inspired a client to share your products or you could have enticed a professional affiliate marketer with a profitable list.

Getting people sent to your sales pages is pretty cool, but giving money to marketers only after they buy from your email list is 1,000x more productive.

Benefit 5: Allows you to make money on demand.

One of the major benefits of owning a list is having access to thousands of ready to buy readers. This will allow you to create new products and sales pitches around time frames that are crucial in business and in life. Without an email list, selling a new product would take time and patience. With an email list, you can complete a sales effort in a few days.

If you need to buy a new car, pick up some extra money for a vacation, or capitalize on a good investment opportunity, you have the chance to throw out a pitch out to people who trust you so you can create some extra cash flow on demand.

Benefit 6: It allows you to casually sell other products.

When you have a website that people casually visit, rapport can turn into a tricky subject. On the other hand, having a list is like owning a broadcast system that allows people from all walks of life join a community through inspiration and similarities.

Unless you're a 30 year veteran in the online business, odds are you won't be able to produce the #1 trusted authority on a subject. However, you can capture a percentage of the market, and then introduce that email list to new authorities. In addition to making some extra cash by selling products, routinely referencing professionals around a topic transforms business owners from high-horsed "gurus" to trusted sources that prospects and clients can trust to do things right.

Benefit 7: It makes sales fun.

A special feeling fills marketers when they have the opportunity to hang out with their prospects rather than extract money from them in a single exchange. Having dozens of points of contacts allows marketers to feel comfortable selling products and to operate in a fashion that they enjoy. When marketing becomes a chance to share stories and have fun, the conversion game changes from an endless pile of statistics and strategies into a passionate job. Once you're in the groove of email marketing, you'll realize telling stories is your job and you'll have a blast thinking of new ways to make more money.

Chapter 2: Making A Lead Magnet

There is no magic bullet in marketing.

Every market and demographic is different. Even inside the heart of the biggest suburbia in the world, there are completely unique people. Children that grow up in the land of suburbia end up having jobs from all walks of life. They become doctors, musicians, lawyers, carpenters, veterinarians, waiters, clerks, fashion designers, entrepreneurs, travelers, artists and coding experts. Families vary in what food they like to eat, what hobbies they enjoy, and what they like to decorate their home with.

In marketing, it's important to understand that every single person is impacted by a series of experiences that only he or she can truly understand. So how in the world do we tap into people's emotions and convince them to take action?

Making Lead Magnets:

Identifying similar traits and emotions inside of your market during the discovery process is the very first step in creating the foundations of lead magnets. In the first book of this series, we gave an in-depth analysis of what creates a successful lead magnet.

If you haven't had a chance to read it, here's a quick list and brief summary of each step to develop a lead magnet.

1. Be Specific

When you're going to acquire an email from your visitor try to be as specific as possible when you're creating your opt-in. This will allow you to convert on a specific topic and will make it easier to sell a related product inside of your email marketing.

2. Provide a silver bullet.

Think of a nice silver bullet that you're marketing into. What topics were really big and what was everyone buzzing about? It's probably best to think of a simple and effective solution for that topic so you can generate a higher number of opt-ins from the same number of viewers.

3. Your opt-in has to quickly fill the needs of your customer.

When a customer gives you permission to send them emails, they're going to want to have a wonderful feeling of "instant" gratification after they exchange some private information to contact you. Even if you have a free course, the first day of your series has to be a home run for your new subscribers.

4. It should be worth a lot.

Just because you're giving away free content doesn't mean that your content should have a free quality to it. Your opt-in page should feel like an unexpected Black Friday for your customers. When they get a hold of it, they should be blown away that they got this content for free.

Types of lead magnets:

-A guide or a free and relevant report:

-Cheat Sheets.

-A Toolkit.

-A resource list.

-A free trial.

-Free Assessments.

-Quizzes

-Access to prestigious surveys.

*A keynote.

Autoresponders are an intricate part of email marketing. However, it is very easy to install opt-in forms into your website. All you have to do is research how to install an opt-in form for your website and follow the steps.

Core Emailing Strategies:

Email can quickly become comprehensive and overwhelming. By following these simple strategies, you'll put yourself in position for your content to be read. That's the first step to creating a client.

What times are most effective inside of email marketing?

It's easy to think that the best time to email a prospect would be in the morning. However, a few studies have suggested that morning opt-in rates can be the worst when they're sent to work. This is likely due to the fact that most people start off their day at work deleting emails in order to start the day off right and to get into a nice working groove.

When it comes to time zones, EST is the most effective time zone to follow. It captures over 45% of the population and the central time zone, which holds 29% of the population, is only an hour behind. Therefore, appropriately 3 out of 4 American consumers are located within an hour time frame. Emails sent around noon to one in the afternoon tend to be the most effective day time open rates, but night time claimed the throne in terms of effectiveness in email marketing.

Monday is the worst day of the week to send an email, Tuesday through Thursday are the most effective days to send out emails, and the weekend tends to see a dip in the number of subscribers who open emails. This has been confirmed by MailChimp's study that concluded Tuesdays and Thursdays were most active for email marketers. In addition, Experian Marketing stated that the best time frame to send emails is around 8-12 PM EST.

Marketing Rules are meant to be broken.

While it's best to start off with statistically sound marketing strategies when you begin testing marketing strategies, the number one rule in business is to split test your results to maximize your open rates, click through rates, and call to action response rates. Try out Friday night emails and see what happens when you send out something on Sunday morning.

7 Tips for Email Marketing:

1. **Personalize the emails you send, but avoid using names.**

Oddly enough, the days of starting an email with someone's name are dead. This is due to increase illegal activities centered around technology. These damaging practices come in the forms of phishing, stolen identities, financial fraud, and blackmail.

Continuously map out your ways to sound friendly and be relevant while you send out emails. After backtesting, you'll discover what personalized phrases work best for your market. For now, you can take advantage by asking questions, sending breaking news content, and relevant reports that readers are interested   in.

2. **Subject lines do matter, but not in the way you'd expect.**

Adestra released a study that declared long subjects lines don't increase email opening rates. Luckily, subjects that are as long as ten characters or less have proven to open up by half   of   the   subscribers.

Every subject strategy should be documented. Factors to test for include length, noun choices, verbal phrases, and reactions to pain points.

3. Make sure your emails are mobile friendly.

Emails that are mobile friendly have consistently proven to be more responsive than emails that are only designed for the computer. Therefore, when sending out your emails, make sure that the email you send is a pleasant experience for mobile and computer users.

4. Giveaway incredible content before you ask for something in return.

5. Test how often you send emails.

The biggest game inside of email marketing is developing customer anticipation and emotional momentum inside of the email series. If you email daily, you may see a massive drop off in email engagement. Only you can find a perfect way to create the best reading experience for your subscribers.

The best rule of thumb in sending an email is making sure that the topic, subject, and content is worth reading to a subscriber. Maybe it's important for you to mail daily, and maybe it's important for you to mail 2-3 times a month!

6. **Segment your email list.**

When you begin developing email lists, you may want to personalize your prospects into groups as quickly as possible. You can do this through using multiple opt-ins, what emails your prospects actually open, what your prospects interact with, and even whether or not they turn into a paying customer. A perfect example of segmenting would occur if the same email was sent to two subscribers who joined the list on the same day. 30 days after subscribing, one customer has taken a keen interest in investing. He's bought a hands-on guide to finding the greatest infrastructure investments during the Trump administration. The second guy stopped opening up emails after the first week. Without segmenting these two drastically different subscribers, you could end up sending them both a sales pitch about a video course on happiness. These strategies could turn out to be extremely ineffective. However, if you sell the investor a guide on coal investment opportunities, he'd be much more likely to invest. In turn, a fire sale on a small priced product would be a suitable sales tactic for the subscriber who hasn't opened up an email in a while.

7. **Test different content strategies.**

While segmenting seems great on the surface, it becomes brilliant if you choose to categorize your lists into sections like:

1. Quiz lovers

2. Social Butterflies(social media fans)

3. Topics opened and engaged

4. Type of content engaged with(video, audio or text)

5. What style of content was engaged with.(interviews, specialized reports, subscriptions, etc.)

The more times a reader engages with your marketing campaigns, the more likely you are to be able to sell them products and services that they truly enjoy. This will make your clients happier while they put more money into your pockets.

Chapter 3: Creating An Effective Sales Pages

Now that we have honed down our conversion efforts into email marketing, we have a marketer's dream. All that's needed to convert subscribers into buyers is a sales page. Like everything else in conversion, it's best to split test your marketing strategies to see what works best over the long run.

It's also important to note that the number one goal when you send subscribers to your sales pages is to have them emotionally pumped up. This can come in the form of fear based tactics like scarcity on your products, chances of war breaking out, depression, and personal anguish. However, these tactics can be combined with excitement, buzz and entertainment around your product. While getting subscribers to hop on over to your sales pages from your email campaigns, it's important to pay attention to two statistics.

1. The opening rate of your emails previously to your sales pitch and the open rate of the email that directly leads to your sale page.
2. The conversion rate of your sales page.

Conversion opportunities lie directly into two basic statistics once you've simplified your marketing life to consist of emails. They include the emotional charge of your prospects in the days leading up to your sales pitch and the capitalization of that emotional charge inside of your sales message. In order to do this, you must have a combination of excitement, entertainment, and education inside of your subscribers.

In short, have fun with your email marketing and send out promotional emails at a nice rate of 10% of your total emails. This will keep your fan base engaged and allow you to space your control over time.

7 Steps to Building a Successful Sales Page.

Step 1: Create a value proposition for your product and business.

Value Proposition

A value proposition is considered gold inside of professional marketing. Every Fortune 500 Company has a powerful value proposition that they provide for their businesses and their products. Value propositions should turn out to be your main headline and sub-headline for every sales page in order to captivate and capture your subscribers. Without one, your sales efforts are doomed in terms of having a good enough conversion to make a healthy living in online sales.

Your value proposition should be a statement on how your service or product is going to benefit your customer. It should clearly define what you're going to do for your ideal customer and why you're going to be better than your competitors.

According to research done by ChartBeat, you could have as little as 5 seconds to capture your viewer's attention enough to hold them long enough to generate a sale. In other words, you'll lose money if you're not able to communicate value by the time your prospects read your headlines.

Let's pretend you're a software-as-a-service company that sells an email marketing tool. When a prospect searches Google for "best free email marketing tool" and clicks on your link, you want them to stay on your website. **Remember, value propositions are all about fulfilling a void inside of your**

clients. Without filling a void, you become static inside of your prospects and your sales messages won't even be able to get through.

The Power of a Value Proposition
Rules in advertising are meant to be broken, but not this one.

You might be saying to yourself, "A value proposition is just a bunch of words, how is that going to improve my business?"
Let's look at Jamaica Inn to demonstrate the potential impact of a powerful value proposition.

Like a lot of other businesses, Jamaica Inn took a hit when the 2008 recession came around. They lost a lot of business and was pushed up against the wall. They had two remaining options. Either they did something differently or let the company die a miserable death. What transpired was an increase in revenue over 50%, but how in the world did they do that?
They ran a value-proposition-centered campaign. Kyle Mais, General Manager at Jamaica Inn, explained that the first thing they did was conduct a marketing audit inside

of their business to understand where they were losing their potential clients. They found that although Jamaica Inn did well in sales via wholesalers and travel agents, they had to redirect their attention back to marketing to their client base. The first thing they focused on was positioning their new marketing campaign to define the value that they brought to their client's experiences.

What resulted was simple, they developed a value proposition that captured their target audience during a recession. It was a simple but powerful statement, "Jamaica Inn, It's Time.". Their new value proposition revolved around this study and the campaign resulted in:
-A 52% increase in revenue during the length of this campaign
-A 50% increase in website traffic in the first year
-An average ratio of 35:1 for total revenue return-on-investment on the pay-per-click campaign

That's the impact of a powerful value proposition.

What goes into a creating a successful value proposition?

A value proposition will be a clear statement of benefits you'll provide, and it can be influential in creating the successful business that you want. But you're probably asking yourself what exactly goes into writing this statement?

Value propositions can come in different forms, but a basic formula will include these four things:

1. Having a captivating headline
2. Also having a driven sub-headline
3. A list of key benefits and pains to plug into the headlines.
4. A powerful image captures your value proposition.

The headline will be the most important component of your value proposition. Studies that were done for eye-checking have shown that people usually look at the headline more than anything else on the page. So your headline should have a quick statement that will sum up the benefit of what you're offering.

One thing you shouldn't do is make your headline too long. Having it short, will quickly grab the viewer's attention, and will then allow them to naturally shift it towards the sub headline. This is where you can be more specific with your explanation for what you'll do for them.

Your value proposition should communicate your benefits quickly, at times, more detailed and specific ideas can be better. If you're wanting to have more details, you can make a list of key benefits or features that are going to speak to your viewer.

After you set up your headline and sub headline, you can select an image that will further emphasize your benefits.

The image you select should be used with intention. Having a picture that is pretty but irrelevant will not do anything to emphasize your value proposition. However, choosing a picture of your product of your product being used would solidify your value proposition.

How you can you make a strong value proposition?

At this point, it should be clear that the need for a strong proposition is essential, but how will you come up with one?

The first step:

You'll need to take a step back to the discovery process and find out which emotions trigger your audience most powerfully. Find that golden gem that everyone is buzzing about and find a way to present that idea in a unique and powerful fashion. This will help shape the language that you'll use to communicate with your audience and help you find out the best selling point of your product.

If you're still having trouble, you can conduct interviews with your prospects and current clients that are willing to share what sparked them to buy your products.

You should go deep into your interviews and answer questions like:

- What are they doing?
- What's their biggest pain point or problem?
- What kind of language are they using?
- And what outcomes are most important to them.

You'll get to find out what your product or service is doing to help in significant ways to help people that you didn't consider before.

The second step:

The second step in the value proposition creation process is creating an ideal buyer persona. Luckily, creating a customer avatar already put you inside of the perfect position to find your ideal buyer. In fact, you already have :)

However, by this point in time, your customer avatar could have the ability to improve. Once again, take a look at what information customers find important and identify behavioral reactions of major pain points and desires. Pay attention to what pain points are frequent throughout your community's social channels, and ask individuals about these topics. When your persona is clearly defined it's going to help you better understand your prospects as human beings, what they value, what drives them, and what they are wanting to be. This will ultimately help you speak with them inside of your value proposition.

Your third step:

Research your competitors. If someone has had a product up for a while, and they consistently drive traffic to that page, that means that it's working wonderfully enough to make money. By analyzing a collection of research from your competitors, you'll begin to identify underlying sales points within your market to become successful. Then all you have to do is to have "imaginary conversations" with your avatars to develop a fine tuned copy of a couple of value propositions. You can even look into similar products to indicate what else your prospects are looking for.

To research your competitors, all you have to do is look at:

1. Google Adwords advertisements while you search for a topic.
2. Major followings on social media and the products that they sell and how they make money.
3. Major blogs that have generated a lot of monthly visitors.

If there are two companies doing the same thing it won't give either of them uniqueness or give prospects a reason to choose one over the other. You'll want to make them choose you over your competitor.

Your fourth step will be to determine the main benefit of your product or service. When you understand your ideal buyer persona and your competitors, it will be time to determine the main benefit of your product.

Even if you might have various reasons to use your product, there's usually one thing that your audience will be interested in.

To help you figure this out, think of this step in terms of the human desires that was stated by Drew Eric Whitman in Cashvertising. There are eight basic human desires:

1. Social Approval
2. Protection and care from loved ones
3. Comfortable living conditions
4. Freedom from danger, pain, and fear
5. Becoming superior
6. Sexual companionship
7. Life extension, enjoyment of life, survival
8. Enjoyment of beverages and food

Nine desires that are learned:

1. Bargains
2. Profit/ Economy
3. Expression of style and beauty
4. Quality/ dependability
5. Efficiency
6. Convenience
7. Cleanliness of surroundings and body
8. To be informed

One desire will speak the most powerfully for your service or product. To have more credibility, you should provide exact details in how you'll PHYSICALLY impact your client's lives. Are you going to help them increase their sales? Or help them save time during their week? When you develop numbers are concrete, it will provide benefits that your prospects can measure and understand.

Step 2: Create a brief sales pitch followed by a call to action.

After you develop the "face" of your product through developing a value proposition, it's time to open up the floodgates that are geared directly towards convincing your prospects that you can impact their lives enough to look to you as their trusted adviser. In this step, you'll be writing anywhere from four to six sentences with the goal to capture sales through impulse. In this section, you should discuss transformations that your clients will experience. It's like checking out highlights for your favorite sports and shows.

This is where you can throw in some creative flow into your sales pitch and develop a unique sales proposition. Find a way to make yourself different from the competition, and to create an experience where your clients actually visualize what it's like to experience your product or service. Subtle tactics to convince clients to step into a life where your product has transformed their lives is considered an extremely effective sales tactic throughout marketing agencies around the world. Before most people buy your products, they imagine what life would be like after they use the product. They analyze how much work it will take, how practical it is, and the results and experience of what life would be like after successfully using your product or service.

Without guiding your customers through the buying process, you'll never be able to capture income. So bust out a powerful set of benefits followed by a detailed and specific call to action. For example, an effective call to action would be, "after clicking the buy button, you'll be redirected to the cart. After you join 1,000 fellow members, you'll gain instant access to your membership area. You'll have instant access to our course so you can double your sales by the end of the week!".

Step 3: Diving into more dynamics of the sales pitch.

After the first call to action, most customers won't be ready to buy. Luckily, they're still on the page and ready to "research" more about your product. This can be a tricky time in marketing, because, throughout this process, some of your customers may have already unconsciously chosen to buy the product. All they need is "rationalized" explanation of why they should buy the product.

In order to keep up the momentum, you're going to need to develop a few key factors that have become the standards inside of the marketing world.

You have your prospects hooked. They're curious, excited and ready to investigate your product more. One of the main steps to doing this is to embed a series of trust signals for your clients. Trust signals can vary, but the major forms of trust can be your connections inside of the industry, your access to crucial information, what websites your business has been featured on, what clients have to say about your business, and what makes you stand out from your competition.

Building Trust

Sometimes, trust can be hard to develop as a new business owner, so you can include what people are saying about your newsletter, what they commented on your websites, and even what other professionals have said about you while you are investing in traffic campaigns.

You can even give out free trials to your website in exchange for honest reviews!

This section isn't the time to unload a dozen reasons to try your sales pitch. All you're doing is looking for a quick and easy way to develop trust. Once you do that, you can move on into a detailed explanation of your products and services.

Explain more about your product or service.

If your readers are still reading, it means they are hooked into your product. Now is the time to unload your product. You can break down the steps inside of your product, give insights to exactly what the product or service does, and even throw out benefits of every strategy inside of your product or service. This will allow your product to develop a detailed map of what the experience is like while going through this product.

*A KEYNOTE: GUIDE YOUR READERS THROUGH THE PRODUCT LIKE THEY'VE ALREADY BOUGHT THE PRODUCT AND ARE GOING ACTUALLY USING THE PRODUCT. This will help eliminate common barriers that occur inside of marketing and will let your clients know exactly what they'll be experiencing as they use whatever you're selling.

This section can be as long as you want, but a major law in marketing is that your descriptions must be as long as necessary, but no longer.

Revisiting trust factor and the call to action:

Now that your prospects are chomping at the bit to get their hands on your product, you can create a nice purchase button and right below it, signal a brief sign of trust. This needs to be a subtle reminder of the fact that you're trustworthy and that other people believe that you're worth investing in.

This section kind of looks likes a call to action sandwich.   It   goes

-Quick call to action

-Quick trust factor

-More   in-depth   call   to   action.

Step 4: Load up on trust factors

Now it's time to throw the kitchen sink into the mix. This is done by sharing as many testimonials, and other trust factors as possible into your mix. You can use long testimonials, advanced analysis on your topics by experts, and other factors that you think will help boost your case to become your soon to be client's trusted adviser.

By using these 4 simple steps, you can create a successful foundation to begin split testing on. Conversion can be extremely complicated, but sticking to the basics presented in this conversion guide, you'll be able to "hack" your conversion rates and curb the amount of time it takes to create a successful online business.

Chapter 4: Split Testing

The Benefits Of Split Testing

After initial research, split testing will become the most important part of running your business. There are a lot of successful ads, and the truth is if you stick with a semi-successful ad without testing it, you could loose yourself thousands of dollars on every campaign you run.

Odds are you've done business with a Fortune 500 company. These companies thrive in split testing, which is considered as the number one rule in optimizing conversion. Conversion isn't built through one and done methods. It takes a systematic approach that requires marketers to test everything from their ads, landing pages, and back-end sales. Split testing is the process of testing multiple ads against each other in order to understand what sparks prospective customers to take the leap of faith necessary to pull out their wallets.

For marketers, having the ability to test something that works for your site and for your visitors in the most hassle free way to do long term business. It may take consistent effort, but the results over a couple years will transform the income of every business. Essentially, that's what split testing is. It's the process of learning how to speak your market's language in the fastest and easiest way possible.

It won't be as complicated as you might think, and here's how you can utilize split testing.

Split testings will start with an easy installation of invisible tracking codes that you can plug into your pages. This installation will load up multiple versions of opt-ins, emails and sales pitches for various sets of visitors to your site. This will allow you to determine exactly how effective one strategy is against another.

Let's say that you have two pieces of content promoting the same page. Split testing gives marketers and online businesses the opportunity to test an opt-in the page using two completely different types of advertising. The first is a curiosity-driven headline and the second is a benefit driven headline. While it's impossible to tell before testing which marketing strategy works best, the use of split testing allows businesses to hone in on exactly triggers prospects to take action.

In fact, after split testing two advertisements, you may stumble into underlying factors that allow you to combine marketing strategies to make pages convert like crazy. Depending on the response you get from each group, you will be able to determine which page had more effectiveness. You can use this information to tailor-fit the needs and desires of your customers and to understand exactly what they care about.

There are different kinds of split tests and choosing the method to use is going to depend on what you're trying to accomplish. In general, there are two foundational split testing methods.

1. A/B Testing

This kind of testing will involve a single element of your page. It can be anything from an image, headline, long-form copy vs. VSL, or anything that you are needing to check.

The goal of A/B testing is to test one add directly against another. The winner takes the throne as the #1 advertisement strategy for your business.

When you test an ad against a former champion, your goal should always try to improve your conversion rates. Analyze opportunities within your best ads and try to use their success to launch a new champion inside of your advertisement. This strategy takes time, but it's a brilliant way to invest time and money.

Multivariate Testing

This kind of testing is one of the most exciting parts of conversion. The multivariate strategy involves testing multiple elements and combinations on one page versus other combinations on another. This includes content placement, sentence structures, sales combinations, website layout, etc. In multivariate testing, any combination of techniques can be combined, restructured and tested.

However, one of the challenges with multivariate testing is that you are going to need a large amount of traffic to get results that are credible. This is something a new website might not have yet, but it's crucial to document this form of testing. After you start generating profits, this method should be your go-to method for advertising.

Period.

Initially, A/B testing will give some insights into what your audience is wanting based on which test was the winner. This testing will make it easier for you to modify elements on your website according to how your audience is wanting it. The A/B testing will tell you easier than Multivariate testing what your visitors want or like based on the results of the test.

Testing takes the guesswork out of marketing.

One of the most important parts of testing is going to be the hypothesis or, in other words, a marketing strategy. Throughout this guide to conversion, a major point of emphasis was that marketing rules are meant to be broken. Every person is different and every traffic source can change the type of prospects you are speaking to. By blindly pushing analytics out the window, you have a shot at becoming a successful long term. But if you split test, the longer you stay in the game, the more money you make. It's that simple.

After you create a conversion rate that makes you money for your business, you can begin to try to improve your profits. This comes through the testing of new marketing strategies that you believe can be successful if you blend it into your new work.

This is called a hypothesis. A marketing hypothesis is a proven marketing theory that you can test to see if it's compatible with your market and sales pitch. These ideas can be major changes like website design, or as subtle as changing tips to tricks inside a value proposition.

An example of a hypothesis would be:

"Curiosity-driven headlines are more likely to

get my audiences to click on blog posts and explore my website."

Split testing a headline that is curiosity driven against your original headline will help you disprove or prove this.

For all we know, headlines that are benefit driven could compel your audience to click on your site and look around. Maybe benefit-driven headlines are what compels your audiences to click on your site and explore it, and all this time, you've been writing copy that's meant to pique their curiosity. On the flip-side, any hypothesis is deemed wrong, you can use the results to create "conversion corrections".

Conversion Corrections

Conversion corrections could save you years of agonizing pain. For example, let's say you split tested 2 opt-in pages. One was curiosity based and the other benefit based. The curiosity base got a conversion rate of .2% and the benefit base had a little bit better rate of .5%. That means that at best, 5 out of 1,000 visitors signed up to your opt-in pages. So you adjust! You think that maybe the problem is the fact that you missed a major pain point, and you retest 5 total pain points of your customers with unique pitches. After all of that work, nothing moves and your still stuck at a horrible opt-in rate. What do you do? Is the market bad? Do you give up?

NO NO NO!

You're a smart business owner. You've done your research, and something is going wrong that's outside of your current perspective. When you find yourself in ruts, look at your competition. How does their website look on opt-in pages? Does the site look more elegant or less elegant than yours? Are they using video while you use words? Is the picture throwing away your hard work?

-In short, conversion correction occurs when you're simply flopping in statistics.

When this occurs take two simple actions to save your business.

1. Look at least a dozen websites inside of one browser and EXTENSIVELY write down exactly what's going on with their marketing strategies.

2. Look at underlying common traits of your competition and see how your advertisement strategies compare. Is the majority of your competition using video? Checklists? Are they giving more detailed opt-ins? Are they capturing your market from a different perspective than you are? Really dive into what's

happening and develop the two most common opt-in strategies to test against each other. Then plug your current advertisements into what your competition is doing and then retest!

You'll likely see a drastic improvement inside of your opt-in rates. Why?
Because by looking at what was successful, you likely created an advertisement that created an experience that was a polar opposite of your original advertising strategies.
The lesson in this is that if something isn't right, don't slowly make subtle adjustments to your ads. Completely implement a polar opposite experience and look at the results. Then test again, and again until you find a medium experience for your results.
Once this occurs, you can try testing subtle changes inside of your sales tactics to boost conversion rates even further.
The first step in conversion is to have a productive foundation to work on. The second step is to engage in captivating clients through your sales pitches.

You will get tangible, credible results.
By back-testing, you will eventually see real live results. This is because you'll learn how to optimize the experience of your customers by consistently trying new ways to connect to them. Conversion is like visiting a foreign country for the first time. You're new to this place, no one can understand you, and you're finding yourself in a position where you'll have to understand them to adapt and survive. The faster you start learning their culture and language, the faster you'll start to learn how to navigate their world.

This kind of scenario applies to split testing on your own website. Consider your website as yourself and the audience you want to visit the foreign country. The faster you start to speak their language, the easier it's going to be to discover how you're able to communicate effectively, this can be tracked by

- Audience engagement
- Site visits
- Clicks

- Revenue

By using the simple yet effective strategies in this guide, you'll make leaps in bounds in creating a very profitable online business. Marketing and conversion are a game that can always be improved on. This is why testing proven fundamental marketing strategies across multiple industries will be extremely effective when they are combined with already successful conversion strategies that your competition is currently using to dominate the market.

Remember to always stay fresh and relevant. Keep up with the trends and try consistently try to make new ads while high levels of emotion are occurring inside of your industry.

And most importantly, back test everything you try!

Have fun, and cheers to a profitable 2017.

BONUS

Click the image or text link below to access your free bonus.

Access: SuccessTornado.Com/Free-Traffic-Marketing.pdf

www.ingramcontent.com/pod-product-compliance
Lightning Source LLC
Chambersburg PA
CBHW071804170526
45167CB00003B/1172